D1411107

Beagle

A Howling Good Time

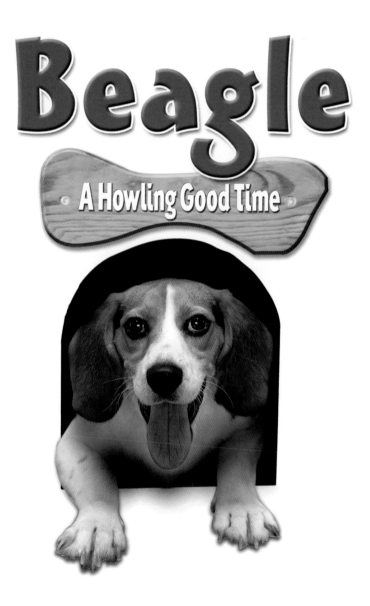

by Duncan Searl

Consultant: Dr. Emily Southgate
Certified Professional Ecologist and Lifelong Beagler

PUBLISHING

New York, New York

Credits

Cover and Title Page, © Datacraft/agefotostock; TOC, © IKO/Shutterstock; 4, © James Tourtellotte/U.S. Customs and Border Protection/Department of Homeland Security; 5, © AP Images/Mike Derer; 6L, © Mario Tama/Getty Images; 6R, © Jack Clark/AGStockUSA/Photo Researchers Inc.; 7, © Mario Tama/Getty Images; 8, © Tom Llewelyn Brewer on his Horse, 'The Doctor', c.1845 (oil on canvas) Artist Mullock, James Flewitt (1818-92)/Newport Museum and Art Gallery, South Wales/The Bridgeman Art Library; 9L, © Elizabeth I, Armada Portrait, c.1588 (oil on panel), Gower, George (1540-96) (attr. to)/Woburn Abbey, Bedfordshire, UK,/ The Bridgeman Art Library; 9R, © Kramer/Info Hund/Photo Researchers Inc.; 10, © Paulette Johnson; 11, © Myrleen Ferguson Cate/Photo Edit; 12, © AP Images/Jason DeCrow; 13, © Kristin Callahan/Everett Collection; 14, © Tristan Hawke/PhotoStockFile/Alamy; 15T, © Gary Randall Photography/kimballstock; 15B, © Henry Ausloos/Animals Animals Enterprises; 16, © Jeff Greenberg/Omni-Photo Communications; 17, © AP Images/The West Central Tribune,Bill Zimmer; 18T, © Tom Nebbia/Corbis; 18B, © James H. Robinson/Photo Researchers Inc.; 19, © David Parket/Omni-Photo Communications; 20, © Karen L. Myers; 21T, © Jill Farley; 21B, © Jill Farley; 22, © USPS/KRT Photo/Newscom; 23, © Time Inc./Time Life Pictures/Getty Images; 24, © Alan Singer/NBCU Photo Bank via AP Images; 25, © Warner Bros./Everett Collection; 26T, © Ron Kimball/kimballstock; 26B, © Jason Lindsey/Alamy; 27, © Pets By Paulette; 28, © George Hoffman/Shutterstock; 29, © Dave King/Dorling Kindersley/Getty Images; 31, © IKO/ Shutterstock; 32, © Anyka/Shutterstock.

Publisher: Kenn Goin
Senior Editor: Lisa Wiseman
Creative Director: Spencer Brinker
Photo Researcher: Amy Dunleavy
Design: Dawn Beard Creative

Library of Congress Cataloging-in-Publication Data

Searl, Duncan.
  Beagle : a howling good time / by Duncan Searl.
    p. cm. (Little dogs rock!)
  Includes bibliographical references and index.
  ISBN-13: 978-1-59716-749-9 (library binding)
  ISBN-10: 1-59716-749-5 (library binding)
  1. Beagle (Dog breed) —Juvenile literature. I. Title.
  SF429.B3S43 2009
  636.753'7—dc22
                    2008037016

For more information, write to Bearport Publishing Company, Inc., 101 Fifth Avenue, Suite 6R, New York, New York 10003. Printed in the United States of America.

10 9 8 7 6 5 4 3 2 1

Contents

A Nose for Trouble

Travelers rushed through Miami International Airport. Before they could board their flights, their bags had to be examined by security officers.

Suddenly, a worker named Trouble sat down in front of a suitcase. He didn't like what he had just discovered.

▲ **Trouble at work at Miami International Airport in 2004**

Trouble is a beagle and one of the airport's most important **employees**. As the top dog in the **Beagle Brigade**, Trouble's sharp nose doesn't miss a thing when sniffing a suitcase.

Why is Trouble at the airport? Sometimes people bring **illegal** fruits and plants into the United States. Insects in those items can cause diseases and ruin crops. Trouble can smell these bugs—even when they are hidden inside luggage.

▲ **Mantis, another member of the Beagle Brigade, alerts his handler to a suspicious suitcase.**

Scientists estimate that a beagle's sense of smell is 1,000 times stronger than a human's.

A Canine Hero

When Trouble sat down after sniffing the suitcase, it was a signal to his **handler**, Sherrie Ann Keblish, that something was wrong. She **seized** the bag and discovered that the fruit inside contained **Mediterranean fruit flies**. If those flies got loose, they could destroy Florida's orange groves!

▲ A Mediterranean fruit fly

In 1997, Florida spent $25 million trying to get rid of Mediterranean fruit flies near the city of Tampa Bay.

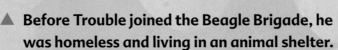

▲ Before Trouble joined the Beagle Brigade, he was homeless and living in an animal shelter.

Protecting the nation's food supply is all in a day's work for Trouble. During his first five years on the job, this friendly little beagle discovered 1,800 dangerous fruits, plants, and meats.

Trouble has been rewarded for his good work. In 2004, this sharp-nosed beagle was voted one of the top **service dogs** in the Canine World Heroes contest sponsored by Pedigree Food for Dogs. He was even honored with a medal at a ceremony in New York City.

◀ **Trouble and his handler, Sherrie Ann Keblish, are shown at the Canine World Heroes ceremony. As part of Trouble's prize, he got his paw prints imprinted in concrete.**

Nothing but a Hound Dog

The Beagle Brigade was formed in 1984, but beagles have been sniffing around for a lot longer. For 8,000 years, people have hunted with large dogs called **hounds**. These dogs use their strong sense of smell to follow the scent of the animals they hunt.

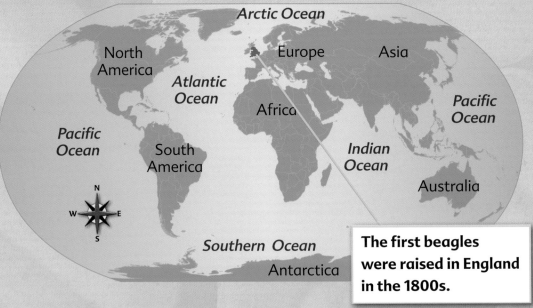

The first beagles were raised in England in the 1800s.

◀ **Hounds on a hunt**

By the 1500s, fox hunting became popular in England. The English wanted dogs that were faster than hounds. So they **bred** foxhounds.

Some English farmers also hunted **hares**. For that, they needed dogs smaller than foxhounds to follow a hare's **scent** under bushes. In the 1830s, English dog breeders first produced beagles like the ones we have today. The small dogs with **keen** noses were perfect for hare hunting.

Foxhound

Queen Elizabeth I

In the 1500s, Queen Elizabeth I of England carried around little dogs that were an early type of beagle. They were called "pocket dogs" because they were so tiny that they fit inside her coat pocket.

Sounds of the Hounds

A beagle's small size isn't the only thing that makes it a good hunter. Its voice is helpful, too.

When a beagle discovers the smell of an animal it's hunting, such as a rabbit, the dog begins to **bay**. This loud, clear **note** tells hunters that the beagle is following the animal's scent.

▲ **A beagle sniffing out a scent**

Beagles were first brought to the United States from England in the 1860s for hunting.

Beagles can **howl** as well. During a hunt, beagles howl to let hunters know when they're close to capturing their **game**. At other times, they just howl for the fun of it.

Like most dogs, beagles also bark and growl at unfamiliar people and things. Their bark may sound scary, but the little hounds almost never bite.

A beagle howling

The Westminster Dog Show

For more than 100 years, thousands of dog lovers from around the world have entered their pets in the **Westminster Dog Show**. This show awards prizes to the top dogs in each breed.

There is also a prize given to the best dog among all the breeds. The 2008 Westminster Dog Show was special for beagle lovers. For the first time ever, a beagle won! Three-year-old Uno was named **Best in Show**.

Handler Aaron Wilkerson leads Uno around the ring during the Best in Show competition.

The little hound was not only the judge's favorite—the crowd loved him, too. Everyone stood up and cheered when he was named the winner. Uno replied with a series of loud "*ah-roos.*"

In 2008, 2,627 dogs competed at the Westminster Dog Show at Madison Square Garden in New York City. In all, there were 169 different breeds.

▲ Since Uno likes to bark, he was also known as the noisiest dog at the show.

A Closer Look

What does a champion beagle look like? Judges at a dog show first check the animal's size.

Beagles come in two official sizes. Small beagles measure 10 to 13 inches (25 to 33 cm) from the ground to their shoulders. They weigh between 18 and 20 pounds (8 and 9 kg). Larger beagles measure 13 to 15 inches (33 to 38 cm) and weigh between 20 and 30 pounds (9 and 14 kg). Beagles bigger than 15 inches (38 cm) cannot compete in most dog shows because they're too tall.

Like all hounds, beagles have muscular shoulders, chests, and legs. They also carry their tails high.

Beagles have long broad ears that hang down. Their ears are too long for their muscles to make them stand up straight like many other dogs.

The judges also check the beagle's **coat**. It should be medium length, thick, and stiff. Most beagles are **tricolored**. This means that they have white, black, and tan markings. Other beagles are only two colors such as red and white or brown and white. A beagle's paws and tail tip are usually white.

Beagles come in many different colors.

A beagle's eyes are large with a gentle look. The nose, mouth, and jaws are straight and square.

The Merry Dogs

Most beagles don't compete in dog shows, but they do make great pets. Few dog breeds are as friendly, happy, and gentle. When early breeders noticed the beagles' good **temperament**, they nicknamed them "the merry dogs."

As pets, beagles love everyone in a family, especially children. Like kids, beagles love to run, jump, and play!

▲ Many people like to adopt beagles from animal shelters because they have such great temperaments.

Beagles make good pets for other reasons, too. They are one of the healthiest breeds of dog, and their small size makes them easy to groom and feed. They are also easy to please. Curious, loyal, and patient, beagles are happy indoors or outside.

▲ Some beagle owners train their dogs to visit nursing homes and hospitals. The gentle, merry little dogs help cheer up patients.

According to the **American Kennel Club**, beagles don't drool or have bad doggy odor.

The Nose Knows

There are many beagles just like Trouble that are working dogs. Agatha Christie from Canada, for example, sniffs out **termites** in basements. When she smells these wood-eating pests, Agatha changes the way she stands. This tells her owner to attack the bugs with chemicals.

Termites

▲ To become a termite-sniffing dog, a beagle needs to complete a 13-week training program.

It's no wonder that Agatha Christie is good at her job. A beagle's nose has more than 220 million **scent receptors**. A human nose has only 5 million.

A beagle's keen nose can be a problem, though. When not on a leash, a beagle can get lost following a scent. Beagle owners need good fences to keep their pets safe!

Along with bloodhounds and basset hounds, beagles have the best-developed sense of smell of any dog.

A-Hunting We Will Go!

Beagles were first bred to hunt with people, and they still hunt with them today. In the United States, many beagle **packs** hunt rabbits, usually once a week, from October through March. In November and April, the National Beagle Club holds large hunting competitions between packs. Both the dogs and their owners enjoy the chase through the beautiful countryside.

During a hunt, beagles travel in packs and follow the directions of a human leader.

▲ **Beagles on a hunt in March 2008**

Another type of hunting, called **drag hunting**, is popular in places such as Victoria, Australia. During these hunts, a strong scent, such as fish oil, is dragged across open land. Uphill and down, the beagles follow the smell. When they make it to the end of the course, they get a treat. Over the past few years, one beagle has often been the leader in these hunts—Davey. He tries to keep the others on track with his loud baying.

The Victorian Beagle Club on a drag hunt

Davey tries to ▶ **find the scent.**

The World's Most Famous Beagle

One of the best-known beagles in the world is the cartoon character Snoopy. Hero of the *Peanuts* comic strip, this little white dog with big black ears has been entertaining people for more than 50 years!

PEANUTS

USA
33

2001

▲ Snoopy is the only beagle to appear on his own postage stamp!

Snoopy first appeared in the *Peanuts* comic strip in 1950.

Snoopy spends most days lying on top of his doghouse. It might not sound exciting, but this little hound has a great imagination. In his mind, he's a heroic pilot, a famous writer, and even an Olympic ice-skater.

Snoopy never speaks, but his face and thought balloons say it all. Everyone knows this brave and happy little beagle is very cool!

◀ **Snoopy and friends**

Underdog

Snoopy isn't the only famous beagle. Other beagles have become stars, too.

The 2007 action film *Underdog* features a beagle in the title role. Underdog gets his superpowers during a lab accident. Like Superman, he never stops fighting the bad guys.

The Underdog balloon during the Macy's Thanksgiving Day Parade in New York City

In 1964, Underdog made his first appearance as a cartoon character in a TV show. Whenever he arrived at the scene of a crime he would say, "There's no need to fear, Underdog is here!"

In *Cats and Dogs*, a popular 2001 film, a beagle named Lou was cast as a secret agent. His job was to stop an evil cat from taking over the world! In the movie, five beagles and one puppet played the part of Lou.

Lou, from *Cats and Dogs*

A Pack of Puppies

Beagle babies are as cute as they come. At birth, the tiny puppies cannot see or hear. After a week or two, their eyes and ears open.

At three weeks, baby beagles begin to walk. After that, there is no stopping them. Even young beagles have keen noses and can sniff out fun, though sometimes their noses get them in trouble.

Beagle mothers take ▶ good care of their pups. The puppies only weigh between 9 and 12 ounces (255 to 340 g) at birth.

◀ Beagles are born with black and white markings. Most of the brown color develops later.

Beagle mothers usually have from three to seven puppies in a **litter**.

When beagles are eight weeks old, they weigh about four pounds (1.8 kg). They are then ready to leave their mothers. Many families want to adopt the puppies. With a beagle, they're sure to have a howling good time!

Beagles at a Glance

	Smaller Beagles	Larger Beagles
Weight:	18–20 pounds (8–9 kg)	20–30 pounds (9–14 kg)
Height:	10–13 inches (25–33 cm)	13–15 inches (33–38 cm)
Coat Hair:	Medium	Medium
Colors:	Mostly tricolored (white, tan, and black); some come in two colors such as red and white or brown and white; others have speckled gray coats	

Country of Origin: England

Life Span: 10–15 years

Personality: Gentle, good-natured, loyal, and curious

Best in Show

What makes a great beagle? Every owner knows that his or her dog is special. Judges in dog shows, however, look very carefully at a beagle's appearance and behavior. Here are some of the things they look for:

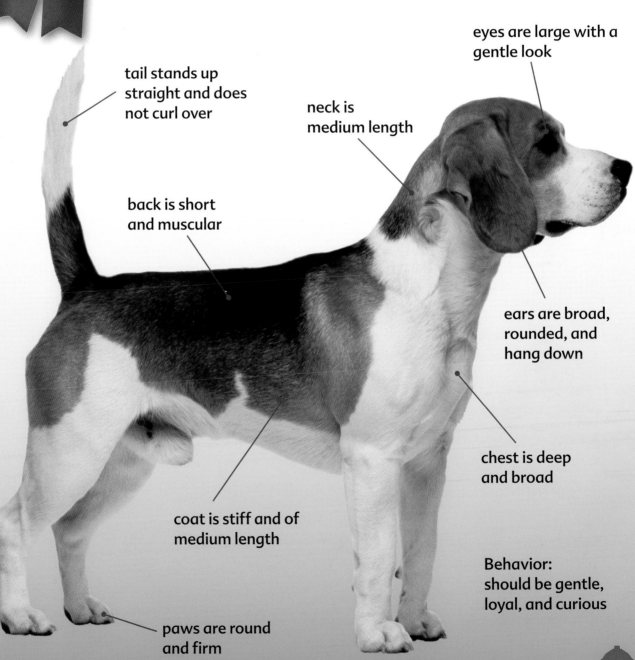

eyes are large with a gentle look

tail stands up straight and does not curl over

neck is medium length

back is short and muscular

ears are broad, rounded, and hang down

chest is deep and broad

coat is stiff and of medium length

Behavior: should be gentle, loyal, and curious

paws are round and firm

Glossary

American Kennel Club (uh-MER-i-kuhn KEN-uhl KLUHB) a national organization that is involved in many activities having to do with dogs, including collecting information about breeds and setting rules for dog shows.

bay (BAY) to make a deep, long songlike bark

Beagle Brigade (BEE-guhl bri-GAYD) a group of beagles trained by the U.S. federal government to detect fruits, vegetables, and meats that carry dangerous diseases and insects

Best in Show (BEST IN SHOH) the top-rated dog in a dog show

bred (BRED) raised for a special purpose

coat (KOHT) a dog's outer covering of hair

drag hunting (DRAG HUHNT-ing) a sport in which a group of beagles follows a scent that has been dragged over the ground

employees (em-PLOI-eez) people or animals who work for another person or business

game (GAYM) wild animals hunted for sport or food

handler (HAND-lur) a person who helps to train or manage a dog

hares (HAIRZ) animals that look like large rabbits and have long, strong back legs

hounds (HOUNDZ) dogs with long drooping ears that hunt by scent

howl (HOUL) to give a long, loud cry

illegal (i-LEE-guhl) against the law

keen (KEEN) very sharp

litter (LIT-urz) a group of animals born at the same time to the same mother

Mediterranean fruit flies (*med*-i-tuh-RAY-nee-uhn FROOT FLYEZ) very destructive flies whose larvae attack fruits and vegetables

note (NOHT) a distinctive sound made by a hunting dog during a hunt

packs (PAKS) groups of dogs kept together for hunting

scent (SENT) a smell or odor

scent receptors (SENT ri-SEP-turz) special cells in the nose that are used for smelling

seized (SEEZD) snatched; grabbed hold of

service dogs (SUR-viss DAWGZ) dogs that are trained to help people

temperament (TEM-pur-uh-muhnt) a person's or animal's nature or personality

termites (TUHR-mites) insects that eat wood

tricolored (TRYE-kuhl-urd) having three colors

Westminster Dog Show (WEST-*min*-ster DAWG SHOH) the yearly dog show of the Westminster Kennel Club

30

Bibliography

The American Kennel Club. *The Complete Dog Book. Twentieth Edition.* New York: Ballantine Books (2006).

Arnold, David, and Hazel Arnold. *A New Owner's Guide to Beagles.* Neptune City, NJ: TFH Publications, Inc. (1998).

Hausman, Gerald, and Loretta Hausman. *The Mythology of Dogs: Canine Legend and Lore Through the Ages.* New York: St. Martin's Press (1997).

Parent, Lucia E. *Beagles: Everything About Purchase, Care, Nutrition, Breeding, Behavior, and Training.* Hauppauge, NY: Barron's (1995).

Read More

De Vito, Dominique. *Beagles.* Neptune City, NJ: TFH Publications (2007).

Kallen, Stuart A. *Beagles.* Edina, MN: Abdo & Daughters (2002).

Rake, Jody Sullivan. *Beagles.* Mankato, MN: Capstone Press (2006).

Learn More Online

To learn more about beagles, visit **www.bearportpublishing.com/LittleDogsRock**

Index

About the Author

Duncan Searl is a writer and editor who lives in New York State.
He is the author of many books for young readers.